INTO HIS PRESENCE
"Study Questions"

Tabernacle & The Priesthood

BOBBY HOLMES

WESTBOW
PRESS®
A DIVISION OF THOMAS NELSON
& ZONDERVAN

WestBow Press books may be ordered through booksellers or by contacting:

WestBow Press
A Division of Thomas Nelson & Zondervan
1663 Liberty Drive
Bloomington, IN 47403
www.westbowpress.com
844-714-3454

Scripture taken from the King James Version of the Bible.

ISBN: 978-1-6642-6690-2 (sc)
ISBN: 978-1-6642-6691-9 (e)

Print information available on the last page.

WestBow Press rev. date: 05/12/2022

Chapter 1

The Law of God and The Tabernacle

1) *What were the two reasons God told Moses to come up into Mount Sinai?*

2) *What was Moses instructed to do when he came up into Mount Sinai?*

3) *In your opinion, what was the purpose of being 6 days early?*

4) *Moses obeyed God and went up into Mount Sinai. What took place in order for Moses to meet God?*

5) *Moses was in Mount Sinai for 40 days and 40 nights. How long was he with God; being shown the Tabernacle and all of its furnishings?*

6) *What specific way was Moses instructed to build the Tabernacle?*

7) *Why was it so important to build the Tabernacle exactly like the one God showed to Moses in the Mount?*

Chapter 2

Who Built the Tabernacle?

1) *What were their names and what did their names mean?*

Chapter 3

How was the Tabernacle Built?

1) *What 4 things did they receive of the Spirit of God?*

2) *Who built the True Tabernacle, chapter and verse?*

3) *How does building the Tabernacle relate to us?*

Chapter 4

The Courtyard Fence

1) *What did the wood post represent?*

2) *What was the post overlaid with and what did it represent?*

3) *What was the curtain attached to?*

4) *What's the Hebrew definition of fillets in Exodus 27:10 (2838)?*

5) *What does the word Filleted (2836) with silver mean in the original Hebrew language, from verse 17?*

6) *Each post had something on top of them. What was it and what did it represent?*

7) *With our study of each part of the Courtyard Fence, write a summary of God's revelation that you can see in the scriptures as you look upon the Courtyard Fence and explain what He's clothed you in.*

(Refer to the first paragraph of the Chapter on the Courtyard Fence)

Chapter 5

The Entrance of the Courtyard

1) *What was the size of the Gate and the Fence on each side of it?*

2) *The Gate being the only way into the Courtyard would remind us of what scripture?*

Chapter 6

The Brazen Altar

1) *The Brazen Altar was made of* _____ _____
and overlayed with _____, *which represents* _____.

2) *What was the size of the Brazen Altar?*

3) *What's the size of the Brazen Altar and the way it was built symbolic of?*

4) *There was a Grate of Network of Brass for the Brazen Altar. Where was the Grate placed?*

5) *What was the Grate of Network of Brass for?*

6) *What did it represent?*

7) *What is the Compass of the Altar?*

8) *When someone brought an offering unto the Lord, who took the life of the animal sacrifice?*

9) *The blood was poured out round about the altar against the Grate of Network of brass and no doubt against the altar itself. What was this symbolic of?*

10) *Knowing the Brazen Altar was hollow on the inside according to Exodus 27:8 and the Grate of Network of Brass was on the outside of the altar, how was the sacrifice placed upon the altar?*

11) *How was the sacrifice placed in order upon the wood and how did they reach that far?*

12) *How was the sacrifice placed in order upon the wood and how did they reach that far?*

13) *What was this symbolic of?*

Chapter 7

The Priesthood

1) *Where is the scripture that says the Priesthood will be established with Aaron and his sons as an everlasting Priesthood and why?*

2) *What was the purpose of the Priesthood?*

3) *Write a summary of what it means to bear the iniquity of the Sanctuary and the Priesthood.*

4) *God gave the Priesthood to them as a service gift. What service was expected of them?*

5) *Tracking the Priesthood down through the generations shown in I Chronicles, chapter 24; the descendants of Aaron. Who is a direct descendent of Aaron according to scripture in the New Testament?*

6) *What Old Testament scripture does this seem to fulfill having to do with the Priesthood?*

7) *Why did John the Baptist baptize Jesus?*

8) *What Priestly Garment was Jesus clothed with?*

Chapter 8

The Church being Consecrated into the Priesthood

1) What did Jesus do with the disciples after supper?

2) What's the overall concept of what is being done here?

3) What Old Testament scripture having to do with the Priesthood do these scriptures remind you of?

4) What type of service does God consider the Priesthood to be?

5) What about those of us beyond the day of the Cross? How are we brought into the Priesthood?

Chapter 9

The Garments of the Priesthood

1) Who was to be clothed in the Garments of the Priesthood?

2) What did God say the Garments were for? (2 purposes)

3) Name the Garments.

4) How was Aaron and his sons hallowed, consecrated into the Priesthood?

5) Did Moses put all the Garments upon them?

6) What does the Linen Breeches and the white linen Broidered Coat represent?

Chapter 10

Garments of the High Priest

1) **What Priestly Garments and other items did the High Priest wear, that the other priest did not?**

2) **How often did the High Priest enter into the Holy of Holies?**

3) **Which Priestly Garments were worn into the Holy of Holies?**

Chapter 11

The Robe of the Ephod

1) What color was the Robe of the Ephod?

2) How was it put on?

3) Did Aaron put this Garment on by himself?

4) Describe the Robe of the Ephod.

5) Where was the Robe of the Ephod worn?

6) What was the purpose of the Robe of the Ephod?

7) What sound was heard and what did it represent:

8) What New Testament chapter is symbolic of the bells and pomegranates on the bottom of the robe?

9) Did the disciples know anything about the day of Pentecost:

10) How many days did Jesus show Himself alive after His resurrection?

11) Jesus told the disciples not to depart from the city of Jerusalem, but to wait for the promise of the Father? What was the promise of the Father?

12) The disciples returned to Jerusalem and gathered in the upper room for the next 10 days. What was this symbolic of?

Chapter 12

The Ephod

1) What was special about the 2 onyx stones on the shoulders of the Ephod?

2) What was the purpose of this?

3) Where was the Breastplate of Judgment placed upon the Ephod?

4) What was the purpose of this?

5) Aaron was to bear the names of the children of Israel before the Lord continually; to carry their load, to bear the judgment. What Old Testament scripture having to do with the Priesthood does this remind you of?

6) What was the Hebrew definition for the Urim and Thummim?

7) Where was the Urim and Thummim placed at on the Ephod?

8) What was the purpose of the Urim and Thummim?

9) Going forward to the New Testament, knowing we have been permitted to wear the Ephod and the Breastplate of Judgment, how is it that we have received the Urim and Thummim to place upon our hearts as we come into the presence of the Lord, not only for ourselves, but also on the behalf of others?

Chapter 13

The Laver

1) **Where was the Laver located?**

2) **What was the Laver made from?**

3) **How often did Aaron and his sons have to wash their hands and feet at the Laver?**

4) **What was washing their hands and feet symbolic of?**

Chapter 14

The Door of the Tabernacle

1) What did the Door of the Tabernacle represent?

2) Why were the 5 sockets that 5 pillars sit on made of brass or copper?

3) What did the 5 pillars covered in gold represent?

Chapter 15

The Tabernacle Structure

1) What type of wood was used to build the Tabernacle and what did it represent?

2) What's the Hebrew definition for Shittim wood and what was the size of each board?

3) What was the foundation that each board sat on, what did it weigh, and what did it represent?

4) What held the boards secure, in place, on the Sockets of Silver and what did they represent?

5) What did this represent?

6) How did the boards sit in order and what did this represent?

7) The Tabernacle was 15 feet wide and Exodus 26:25 says there were 8 boards and 16 sockets of silver on the west end; the backside. The boards were 18 inches wide. How did they make this work?

8) What did the two 9" boards represent?

9) There were 16 Sockets of Silver, two sockets under every board and according to Exodus 38:27 each Socket of Silver was made of one talent of silver, which is 75 pounds. How did they make this work for the two 9" boards in the corners?

10) The two corner boards were to be Coupled Together (8382) beneath and coupled together above the head of it unto one ring. What was the purpose of this and what did it represent?

11) The Tabernacle was 15 feet tall, sitting on solid blocks of silver. What kept the boards all in line and straight with one another towards the top and what did this represent?

Chapter 16

The Lampstand

1) What was the Lampstand and the vessels they used made from?

2) What was the Lampstand used for; what purpose?

3) What scripture references relates the Lampstand to the Word of God?

4) Some of the ornaments were shaped like unto almonds. What does this represent?

5) How many ornaments were in the Lampstand and what do they represent?

6) What was special about the shaft of the Lampstand, what was its purpose and what did it represent?

Chapter 17

The Table of Shewbread

1) What was the Table of Shewbread made from and overlaid with what? What did this represent?

2) What is the border of the Table of Shewbread? What is it for and what does it represent?

3) The Table of Shewbread was made of wood overlaid in gold, but the dishes thereof were made of pure gold. Why was this and what did it represent?

Chapter 18

The Golden Altar

1) What was the Golden Altar made from and overlaid with? What did this represent?

2) What was the purpose of the Golden Altar and what did it represent?

3) Where did the Golden Altar sit at within the Tabernacle?

4) How was the Golden Altar carried throughout the wilderness? How was it supported and what did it represent?

Chapter 19

The Incense

1) What is the name of the sweet spices that were used to make the Incense?

2) How was the mixture of the spices to be used?

3) What was the name of the profession of mixing these together?

4) God gave the mixture of Incense a name. What was it and what did it represent?

Chapter 20

The Holy Place

1) What was another name for the Holy Place?

2) What furniture was placed within the Holy Place and what was this symbolic of?

3) What furniture was placed within the Holy Place and what was this symbolic of?

Chapter 21

The Tabernacle Coverings

1) What was the size of the Tabernacle?

2) What was the size of the first inner covering?

3) How many curtains made up the inner covering?

4) How many curtains covered the Holy Place and how many covered the Holy of Holies?

5) How were the curtains connected together and what did this represent?

6) Where did the 5 curtains over the Holy Place connect to the 5 curtains over the Holy of Holies?

7) **How were the 5 curtains over the Holy Place connected to the 5 curtains over the Holy of Holies and what did this represent?**

Chapter 22

The Veil

1) What was the purpose of the Veil?

2) What was the Veil attached to? What was its foundation and what did this represent?

3) There were 50 loops of blue that joined the Holy Place to the Holy of Holies, just above the Veil. What did this represent?

4) What does the red color of the Veil represent?

5) How did they get the scarlet (8144, 8438), red color?

Chapter 23

The Placement of the Veil

1) The veil represented Jesus' body and separated the Holy Place from the Holy of Holies. Why was this needed in order for God to dwell among His people?

2) When Jesus died upon the Cross, what took place in the Temple and what did this represent?

3) We have been given access into the very presence of God by the blood of Jesus; all sin has been forgiven, the power of sin has been broken, and we have been redeemed and the Spirit of God lives within us. What other blessing / benefit have we received because of the blood of Jesus; to cause us to be able to serve the Living God?

Chapter 24

The Ark of the Covenant

1) What was the Ark of the Covenant made of and what did it represent?

2) It was overlaid with pure gold within and without. What did this represent?

3) What New Testament scripture would this reflect upon?

4) What was kept inside the Ark of the Covenant and what did they each represent?

5) Understanding question #4, what is this promise of God we've been given in the Old Testament Tabernacle?

6) What's the name of the lid of the Ark of the Covenant and what does it represent?

Chapter 25

The Journey through the Wilderness

1) How did the children of Israel know when it was time to disassemble the Tabernacle and move?

2) What was done first in the disassembling the Tabernacle and who did it?

3) There were 6 wagons and 12 oxen given unto the Levites for the service of the Tabernacle, but none was given unto the sons of Kohath, because the service of the Sanctuary belonging unto them was that they should bear upon their shoulders. They were to carry the Ark of the Covenant, Table of Shewbread, Laver and the Brazen Altar. What was the purpose of this and what did it represent?

Printed in the United States
by Baker & Taylor Publisher Services